ONCE UPON A DREAM

Amazing Poets

Edited By Lynsey Evans

First published in Great Britain in 2024 by:

YoungWriters Est. 1991

Young Writers
Remus House
Coltsfoot Drive
Peterborough
PE2 9BF
Telephone: 01733 890066
Website: www.youngwriters.co.uk

All Rights Reserved
Book Design by Ashley Janson
© Copyright Contributors 2024
Softback ISBN 978-1-83565-471-2
Printed and bound in the UK by BookPrintingUK
Website: www.bookprintinguk.com
YB0591J

FOREWORD

Welcome Reader, to a world of dreams.

For Young Writers' latest competition, we asked our writers to dig deep into their imagination and create a poem that paints a picture of what they dream of, whether it's a make-believe world full of wonder or their aspirations for the future.

The result is this collection of fantastic poetic verse that covers a whole host of different topics. Let your mind fly away with the fairies to explore the sweet joy of candy lands, join in with a game of fantasy football, or you may even catch a glimpse of a unicorn or another mythical creature. Beware though, because even dreamland has dark corners, so you may turn a page and walk into a nightmare!

Whereas the majority of our writers chose to stick to a free verse style, others gave themselves the challenge of other techniques such as acrostics and rhyming couplets.

Each piece in this collection shows the writers' dedication and imagination – we truly believe that seeing their work in print gives them a well-deserved boost of pride, and inspires them to keep writing, so we hope to see more of their work in the future!

CONTENTS

All Faiths Children's Academy, Strood

Ella-May Simpson (8)	1
Aliya Briant (8)	2
Lillian Clarkson (8)	3
Olivia Watson (8)	4
Ronnie-Roy Burdett-Mckenna (7)	5
Emma Drury (8)	6
Phoebe Woollcott (7)	7

Burnley Lowerhouse Junior School, Burnley

Olivia Rothwell (10)	8
Eliana Barker-Smith (9)	10
Marli Eddy (9)	12
Destiny Ashe (10)	13
Florence Horsfall (9)	14
Finley Broadhurst (9)	15
Sophie Tomlinson (9)	16

Castlefield Primary School, Greenhills

Aaron McGurl (10)	17
Max Tobin (10)	18
Luke Moffat (9)	20
Luke Powell (10)	21
Blair Wilson (10)	22
Israel Ajayi (10)	23
Ibrahim Amodu (10)	24
Chloe Robinson (10)	25
Jacob Kirkwood (10)	26
Leila Stirling (9)	27
Isaac Ajayi (10)	28

Aaron Cook (10)	29
Cole Gillies (9)	30
Curtis Mundt (9)	31
Liam Neilson (11)	32
Ellie Smith (10)	33
Jay Doherty (10)	34

Mesne Lea Primary School, Worsley

Millie Mrowiec (9)	35
Louis Molyneux (9)	36
Juliet Kerns (9)	37
Harrison Seddon (9)	38
Eseosa Ogbe (8)	39

Mossford Green Primary School, Barkingside

Wafiq Chowdhury (11)	40
Maghizhini Manikandan (10)	42
Aleena Choudhury (10)	44
Elias Thawe (10)	45
Zaynab Ali (11)	46
Sanda Bargan (11)	47
Michelle Naing (10)	48
Amaiya Patel (10)	49

Oldcastle Primary School, Bridgend

Izzy Phipps (9)	50
Amelia Parfitt (8)	51
Eloise Jones (9)	52
Hattie Lancett (9)	53
Fara Docherty (9)	54

Lottie Thomas (9)	55
Effie John (8)	56
Oona Taylor (9)	57
Sofia Hearne (9)	58
Bette George (9)	59
Heidi Baldwin (9)	60
Maisy Leah Robinson (8)	61
Gracie Rose Pring (8)	62
Violet Powell (8)	63
Isla Evans (8)	64

Pheasey Park Farm Primary School, Great Barr

Elliott Seeley (8)	65
Joshua Anderson (9)	66
Bethany Fisher (9)	68
Harry Myatt (9)	69
Hameedah Shaibu (9)	70
Lily Rose Farley (9)	71
Benjamin Hampshire (8)	72
Isla Titchen (8)	73
Sienna Dunn (9)	74
Karis Chan (9)	75
Niamh Guilfoyle (9)	76
Minnie McKeown (8)	77
Bella-Louise Reynolds (8)	78
Erica Melintescu (8)	79
Seren Thomas (9)	80
Eva Barclay (9)	81
Josette Yue (9)	82
Evie-Rose Barrowclift (9)	83
Victoria Saskowska (9)	84
Toby Boekbinder (9)	85
Sofia Chen (9)	86
Erin Summlar (9)	87
Isabelle Taylor-Brown (9)	88
Harvey Wilde (8)	89
Juliette Boreham (8)	90
Riley Lander (9)	91
Simreet Kaur (9)	92
Benjamin Wacogne (8)	93
Chikamdinaka Ugochukwu (8)	94
Arun Kumar-Ford (9)	95

Lillie O'neill (9)	96
Aria Law (8)	97
Jay Smith (8)	98
Elliott Anderson (8)	99
Addison Webb (8)	100
Ted Seeley (8)	101
Paige Johnson (8)	102
Thea Hadgkiss (8)	103
Amelia Forrester (8)	104
Dylan Bhopla (9)	105
Serenity Bartholomew (8)	106
Olivia Bland (9)	107
Esmae Hollyhead (8)	108
Drew Wheller-Grice (8)	109
Mikaeel Puri (8)	110
Ella-Rose Darby (8)	111
Hafee Siddiqui (9)	112
Olivia-Rae Byrne (8)	113
Alfie Heath (9)	114

Potton Primary School, Potton

Cassie Desborough (9)	115
Emilia Phillips (9)	116
Amber Schultz (9)	118
Aina Roberts (8)	119
Akorede West (8)	120
Ellie Elias (9)	122
Kayla Garrett (8)	123
Sakina Duggal (9)	124
Ava-Mai McCarthy (8)	125
Brooklynn Donegan (8)	126
Nathan Cornwall (9)	127

Sunninghill Preparatory School, South Walks

Emily Platt (8)	128
Sonny Hamlin (8)	129
Freya Holland (7)	130
William Kerr (7)	131
Alice Wright (8)	132
Beauden Mudge (7)	133
Daisy Baker (8)	134

Wath C Of E Primary School, Rotherham

Lily Atkinson (9)	135
Isobel Foley (10)	136
Alice Ashley (10)	138
Riley Fitzgerald (10)	140
Harry Kittle (10)	141
Maisie Lloyd (9)	142
Josh Chandler (10)	143
Poppy Edwards-Ratcliffe (10)	144
Charlie Hickling (9)	145
Viviana Exton (10)	146
Grace Foley (10)	147
Ellie Needham (10)	148
Reuben Hatton (10)	149
Ruby Heppenstall (9)	150
Jacob White (9)	151
Effie Luana Murphy (9)	152
Oliver Bankes (9)	153
Lucas Wilby (10)	154
Harley May-Straw (10)	155
Leo Rook (10)	156
Lily Tyler (9)	157
Harry Thompson (9)	158
Luke Coxon (9)	159
Sebastian Platts (10)	160
Louis Edwards (9)	161
Isobel Phillips (10)	162
Blake Stone (10)	163
Alicia Henderson (9)	164
Jacob Smith (9)	165
Finley Cole (9)	166
Sonny Blood (9)	167
Maddie Boothroyd (9)	168
Seb Dunn (10)	169
Freddie Bell (10)	170
Keelan Nkomo (9)	171
Owen Hanson (9)	172
Brody Buck (10)	173
Thomas Pearson (9)	174
Alexander Brough (9)	175
Jorgie Auckland (9)	176

West End Primary And Nursery School, Horsforth

Rosie Ibbo (9)	177
Lia Brewitt (9)	178
Emily Berry (9)	180
Pia Terry (9)	181
Seth Morton (9)	182
Freya Gawthorpe (9)	183
Polly Munson (8)	184
Ryder Kwok (9)	185
Isobel Barnes (8)	186
Sienna Christou (8)	187
Polly Bagnall (9)	188
Ethan Taylor (9)	189
Harry Pearson (9)	190
Holly Adams (9)	191
Ayda Solhan (9)	192
Josh Wheat (9)	193
Dylan Thorpe (8)	194
Charlie Buckle (8)	195
Jacob Barker (8)	196
Jack Hollowood (9)	197
Elliot Johnson (9)	198
Charlotte Wood (9)	199
Liv Gallagher (8)	200
Toby Bagnall (9)	201
Charlie Banks (8)	202
Ellen Procter (9)	203
Florence Hoult (8)	204
Reuben Barker (8)	205
Jake Petty (9)	206

THE POEMS

The Ten Friends

D ark at night in the moonlight
R unning in the night, so scared with my nine friends
E veryone is in their beds, but just the ten of us are awake
A fter midnight still awake, tired and scared
M onsters stomping and roaring in the dark and I'm so scared.
S oon I fell asleep for an hour when I woke up in a dream.

Ella-May Simpson (8)
All Faiths Children's Academy, Strood

My Fear

My name is Aliya, I dream of going up the Shard.
My fear is heights, so this is hard.
I always think about facing my fear.
I want my scaredness to disappear.
Maybe I'll go with my family.
They'll encourage me happily.
After days and days, my dream came true.
It finally happened, and I said, "Phew!"

Aliya Briant (8)
All Faiths Children's Academy, Strood

Little Creeps

Once there was a pitch-black shadow
The shadow was narrow
And so in my creepy dream
There was no sight of light
I see shiny bright.
It's that that gives me a creepy fright.
Such no place to be.
I really am in a creepy clown dream
The spiders got to my room
And in the stinky loo.

Lillian Clarkson (8)
All Faiths Children's Academy, Strood

Dreams

D ark in the night the monster crept in the moonlight
R unning outside and running into my bed
E very fright gets to me at night
A fter midnight I start to get a fright.
M y night starts to give me a creep while I sleep
S oon I wake up and realise, it's a dream.

Olivia Watson (8)
All Faiths Children's Academy, Strood

Getting Lost

I am lost. Lots of spiders and monsters are going for a walk.
Everything seems so quiet and slow.
Trees are whistling as I walk.
Ahh, out pops a monster
So I run faster and faster
Until I have to stop.
I look around to check behind me
Out pops a spider that's trying to bite me.

Ronnie-Roy Burdett-Mckenna (7)
All Faiths Children's Academy, Strood

Dreams

D ark at night gives me a fright,
R unning across the floor at night.
E very one asleep quietly in their beds,
A fter midnight, I am very scared.
M onsters crawling under my bed,
S oon, I'll wake up and see it's a dream.

Emma Drury (8)
All Faiths Children's Academy, Strood

Creep

Creep upstairs, dark at night.
Running up in bed and under.
I run upstairs and have a fright.
I have a fright outside.
Something in the moonlight.

Phoebe Woollcott (7)
All Faiths Children's Academy, Strood

Backwards Circus

My family is on holiday
It's a summer treat
It was a lot to pay

For a surprise
We are going to the circus
And Dad had all the supplies!

A clown called Devastation
He was so upset
He was diagnosed with annihilation.

Then an acrobat with wings
One, then two, then four!
But they were scared out of all things, scared!

A poof of magic appeared
A bunny magician with a man in his hat
In a clown car that was not being steered!

Running
Leaping
The bearded lady had no beard
How stunning!

We stopped for popcorn, yum
Candyfloss and *pop!*
Give me some!

Now we're in our seats!
The showman appears!
He is so boring, talking about meats!

A lion with a tophat!
Holding a hoop
Alfie said, "Purple mane cat!"

Dreams are super cool!
You can do anything!
Like being in a celebrity pool!

Time to wake up!
Now it's school time
I should get my
Favourite cup!

Olivia Rothwell (10)
Burnley Lowerhouse Junior School, Burnley

The Underwear In The Mythical World

I could see a bluebird,
A waving tree.
I could be outside,
Sometimes with my friend, Suzy.
In my world, there's something bright,
Even in the day and the night.
I know the magic doesn't seem there,
Finley chasing his dad's underwear.
So if you want to have a try,
If you want to sleep at night,
If you feel like everything's unfair
Try imagining Finley chasing different underwear.
In this world, you can be whatever you want
A fluffy cat
Or a small rat
Or a sneaky dog.
Look, a running strawberry by the log.
If you like fluffy cats, this poem is for you.
Finley's dad's chasing his underwear.
So if you have a fright
It would probably be at night!

If you want to control your dreams
Join Finley's underwear team!

Eliana Barker-Smith (9)
Burnley Lowerhouse Junior School, Burnley

Time Travelling Into Tudor Past

One day, I travelled to see the Tudors,
Britain's biggest feuders.
Elizabeth the 1st shook my hand,
There was a maiden watering the land.
I curtsied to Henry the 8th,
Oh my gosh, I had faith!
Elizabeth's sister called Mary,
Now I know why they think she ruled as scary,
As scary as a hairy fairy.

They showed me to a room
With a nice red door,
When you walked in
You knew they weren't poor.
The bed gleamed,
I filled up with amazement and laughter,
Then I stared at the room around me after.
At tea, I declared I had a blast,
Wandering about the wonderful past,
And I knew this visit wouldn't be my last!

Marli Eddy (9)
Burnley Lowerhouse Junior School, Burnley

Therianthrophy

Something is being told in the woods;
Aisles of shadow lead away; a branch waves.
A pencil of sunlight slowly travels its path;
A withheld presence almost speaks but then retreats.
Rustles a patch of bush; you can feel centuries ripple,
Generations of wandering, discovering,
Being lost and found.
Eating, dying, being born,
A walk through the forest strokes your fur,
The fur you no longer have.
You gaze down a forest aisle,
Strange, long, plunge dark eyes,
Looking for a home.
For delicious minutes,
You can feel your fangs,
Sharper than your claws,
Away at everything...

Destiny Ashe (10)
Burnley Lowerhouse Junior School, Burnley

My Dancing Alien And Me!

Here is my best friend who loves dancing
He is very silly and the truth is his name is Billy.

Billy likes to go dancing at night
And his heart is a true light.

He has his own mind inside of mine
I think you'll find!

He is amazing for my imagination
He is there for me in any type of situation

I love my alien friend
We will be together at the end

He has other hobbies too
And I think he would love to do them with you!

Florence Horsfall (9)
Burnley Lowerhouse Junior School, Burnley

A Boy And The Cheese Moon

In my dream, every night,
A boy takes a flight.
He takes his dog to the moon,
I'll be going there very soon.

Something wasn't right,
What I saw was a weird sight.
The ground was yellow with holes,
I looked down at an alien holding a bowl.

He asked me to keep a secret, please,
That the moon was made of cheese.
In my dream, every night,
A boy takes a flight.

Finley Broadhurst (9)
Burnley Lowerhouse Junior School, Burnley

Nightmares!

N ever have I experienced something as horrible as this.
I sit as my eyes bawl.
G hosts are my weakness,
H elp, help, I call!
T ight spaces are the worst!
M ay not come out at this time.
A lways wondering when it will end.
R emembering it's not real.
E nding nightmares is always the best, especially when I'm doing it with you!

Sophie Tomlinson (9)
Burnley Lowerhouse Junior School, Burnley

The Terrifying Apocalypse

The apocalypse started before I woke up,
I tried to move, but I knew I was stuck.
I tried to turn, but I was made of stone,
And that was when I heard a deep groan.

I was terrified, scared and full of fear,
I focussed my eyes; a zombie was near!
I smelled its disgusting breath on my face,
And without warning, it started to chase!

Suddenly, the rock split and I was free,
My heart rejoiced; my face was filled with glee!
I thought I was safe, out of harm's way,
No longer its victim, no longer its prey.

As I fled from the zombie's rapid advance,
It reached out and bit me into a trance.
My eyes fluttered open in sleepy dread,
I woke up to find I was safe in my bed!

Aaron McGurl (10)
Castlefield Primary School, Greenhills

Food For Thought

On a dark, dim night, we ventured out,
In the middle of a forest, we found a dugout.
Hesitantly, we pulled back the bushes
And opened the door,
Made our own way down the stairs
And onto the floor.

The lab had been there, totally untouched,
In total amusement, our mouths we clutched.
Upon the shelf were rows of jars,
Filled with delights from afar.
Pink, green and also blue,
"Why don't we eat them? There's only a few!"

Red came first and up we shot,
Standing like giants, or so we thought.
Green was next and soon we were small,
It's crazy how the mighty fall.

Third was pink and disappeared,
How do we get home is what we feared.
Finally, we dared to try the blue,
All of us came back into view.

We stood there wondering what just happened,
If our parents found out, we would be chastened.
We started to leave, back up the stairs,
Step by step, leaving our nightmares.

Max Tobin (10)
Castlefield Primary School, Greenhills

The Mysterious Spaceship

I open my eyes.
I feel disorientated.
I look around curiously.
A giant keyboard of controls stares back at me.
I peer through a small window at the stars in the distance.
The hairs on my back bristle in fear.
I turn my head slowly and there it is...
Its metal armoured coat reflects my rising panic.
What should I do?
Run and hide?
Stay and fight?
The decision is no longer mine!
It lunges towards me full of menace.
It reaches out with its claw-like talons.

I feel its grip on my shoulder.
This is it! Does my life end here?
My senses jolt and I'm fully awake.

"Morning, Luke, it's time for school."

Luke Moffat (9)
Castlefield Primary School, Greenhills

School's Under The Dreams

Deep in sleep, my thoughts run free.
Where will my imagination take me?
Behind my lashes new worlds await,
Lie back, relax and accept my fate.

Tonight, I see a ghostly ghoul,
As it floats around an abandoned school.
Was it a child from days gone by?
What makes it remain? What makes it cry?

Wailing whispers echo down the hall,
As phantom teachers make the call.
To teach lessons of the distant past,
How long can they make this lesson last?

And as dawn breaks, these ghouls retreat,
My body refreshed, a new day to greet.
And when it ends, I'll dream once more,
Of yet another world, I'm sure.

Luke Powell (10)
Castlefield Primary School, Greenhills

The Arcade

As I looked around, fear filled my face,
Silence lingers in the now vacant space.
Once filled with laughter, lights ablaze,
Now shadows dance in forgotten days.

Rows of games now gathering dust,
Tokens lost, dreams turned to rust.
The neon signs, flickering low,
Tell stories from long ago.

Empty chairs, screens gone dark,
Memories fade like a flame's spark.
Through the stillness, a ghostly hum,
Whispers of kids who used to come.

I woke up in the warmth of my bed,
Realising it was all in my head.
A scary dream of a haunted arcade,
Thoughts of my nightmare began to slowly fade.

Blair Wilson (10)
Castlefield Primary School, Greenhills

Fear To Fantasy

In the dead of night, a nightmare crept,
Filling my head as I lay and slept.
The sky was dark and the trees were tall,
I stood in fear, I felt so small.

But suddenly, the trees were parted,
The sun shone bright and gleaming started.
Colours bright like a painted scene,
Replacing the darkness, washing it clean.

Fields of gold and skies so blue,
I screamed with joy, the nightmare through,
As morning came, I woke with glee,
The nightmare gone, I felt so free.
From the dark, light did gleam,
My nightmare turned into a lovely dream.

Israel Ajayi (10)
Castlefield Primary School, Greenhills

The Haunted Hotel

In a haunted hotel where shadows dance,
Whispers creep in at every glance.
Creaking floors and doors that groan,
In this place, you're never alone.

Ghosts roam halls in the dead of night,
Flickering lights fill me with fright.
Guests check in but never leave,
Bound to this place where monsters weave.

If you spend a night in this space,
Your body will shake and your heart will race.
I sprung awake and opened my eyes,
In my own bed, home and alive.
A horrible dream of a haunted hotel,
The nightmare had me under a spell.

Ibrahim Amodu (10)
Castlefield Primary School, Greenhills

Waterpark Dream

In sleep's embrace, I have a waterpark dream,
Where laughter flows in an endless stream.
Slides twist and turn in an exciting way,
As splashes of joy light up the day.

Gentle snores roll like waves on the sea,
Children splash in pools filled with glee.
But this pool is not the normal azure blue,
My dream pool is more of an indigo hue.

It's not the sunbeams that light my way,
But the stars of the galaxy in a beautiful way.
And as I slide down, the end is in sight,
The dawn breaks around me and steals the night.

Chloe Robinson (10)
Castlefield Primary School, Greenhills

The Adventure Of Nightmares

N ight hits and the howling of monsters awaits you.
I feel the panic rush.
G o, go, go! A man screams, "They're coming."
H owls filled the air as they attacked animals and destroyed homes.
T he streets turned red while the monsters walked around.
M en ran for their lives.
A woman cried at the baby she lost.
R unning across the road, my head started to hurt.
E ventually, I closed my eyes in fear.
S uddenly, I heard an alarm, not the monster's alarm, but mine...

Jacob Kirkwood (10)
Castlefield Primary School, Greenhills

The First Dance

I remember it well, that very first chance,
I walked through the door; I wanted to dance.
The floor was smooth, the lights were bright,
The butterflies in my tummy, I had to fight.

I go to class week after week,
New steps, new moves, is what I seek.
I twirl, I leap, I also spin,
The competition I aim to win.

My dream, it burns inside of me,
A professional dancer is what I'll be.
In a West End show, I'll dance the lead,
No one will stop me; I will succeed!

Leila Stirling (9)
Castlefield Primary School, Greenhills

Night In A Gloomy Forest

Deep in my dream, in a forest's gloom,
Where monsters howl and whispers loom,
Amongst the trees, shadows creep,
A nightmare prowls when I'm asleep.

Eyes gleam in the dark night,
Every rustle fills me with fright.
Ghosts wander, heart beating fast,
In this haunted forest where shadows last.

But morning breaks and night will flee,
Leaving this dream as a memory.
Of a dark forest where monsters stay,
Next time I sleep, I'll stay away.

Isaac Ajayi (10)
Castlefield Primary School, Greenhills

Daydreamer

D istant hills beyond the classroom window.
A sky filled with fluffy white clouds.
Y esterday's rain being dried by the sun.
D ancing birds in the blue sky above.
R unning through fields of green.
E verywhere is a chance to explore.
A nywhere except here.
M y mind floats back to the room I'm in.
E scape from reality no more.
R eturning to my jotter and the work to be done.

Aaron Cook (10)
Castlefield Primary School, Greenhills

The Galaxy

T he astronauts are floating around with aliens.
H ow did I get here? Maybe a rocket ship?
E ndless skies with millions of stars shooting aimlessly.

G alaxies miles from this one!
A liens are taking over the Earth!
L ost in space.
A liens everywhere you look.
X -ray vision, they see straight.
Y ou can't escape them... unless you open your eyes.

Cole Gillies (9)
Castlefield Primary School, Greenhills

Hospital

H olding my friend's hand
O pening the door to an abandoned hospital
S potting a bed with a white cover
P etrified, I walk over to it
I reached to lift it but nothing was there
T he demons pulled me back out of the room and my dream
A tear fell from my eye as I realised my friend was gone
L ife will never be the same again.

Curtis Mundt (9)
Castlefield Primary School, Greenhills

Stadium Of Dreams

In vast stadiums, dreams take flight,
Where ambitions grow under floodlights.
With each kick, a journey begins,
In the pursuits of glory, where legends win.

Through practice, hard work, sweat, and tears,
Young players keep going and persevere.
Their skill and dedication pave the way,
For generations to shine in the future one day.

Liam Neilson (11)
Castlefield Primary School, Greenhills

Singing

S inging softly soothes my soul,
I nside, I feel incredible.
N othing near me disturbs my peace,
G leeful grins do not cease.
I mmersed in instruments, I feel so free,
N ew jobs I hope will come to me.
G ood vibes, great beats and tunes galore,

Let's hope I sing forever more.

Ellie Smith (10)
Castlefield Primary School, Greenhills

Nightmare

N asty
I nvaders
G hosts
H orrible
T rolls
M onsters
A ngry
R ats
E vil.

Jay Doherty (10)
Castlefield Primary School, Greenhills

The Room Of Fears

I find myself in a room.
A quiet, empty room.
Whatever it is, I shall explore.
I hear creaking noises beneath my feet.
This is an old place for such a young me.
I spot a wardrobe in front of me
I decide to see whatever is there.
I open the door with a deep breath
And put my foot inside of it.
As I walk inside I notice something,
It is a growling sound near me.
What could it be? It could be anything.
Suddenly I see fur in the distance.
Could it be a creature?
When I looked at it...
I quickly noticed it was a monster!
A scary one!
He chased me out and never gave me back.

Millie Mrowiec (9)
Mesne Lea Primary School, Worsley

The Golden Boot

I walked onto the pitch, unaware of what was happening.
I looked down at my feet, the boots were so dazzling,
As I dribble the ball past Messi and Mbappé,
I shoot, I score, this makes me very happy,
The game is almost over, as I score the winning goal,
I wake up from my dream,
I'm in the winning team.

Louis Molyneux (9)
Mesne Lea Primary School, Worsley

I'm Dancing In My Football Boots

Strange it is,
I've left my home,
I'm in a class, but all alone,
I'm dancing in my football boots,
How strange is that,
Others appear,
And start to laugh,
As I rat-a-tat-tat,
I'm dancing in my football boots,
How strange is that,
They're all sat,
Laughing at that.

Juliet Kerns (9)
Mesne Lea Primary School, Worsley

The Banana Story

I had a dream that bananas
Were jumping on my head and my dog's body!
They always do it
And once a banana went up my dog's nose,
And he started to sneeze.
Then I woke up laughing, "Ha, ha."
This is so funny, I love it.

Harrison Seddon (9)
Mesne Lea Primary School, Worsley

Princess

If I am a princess of royalty
I will have to have maturity
If I want to be kind
I will have to do it with my mind
When I have to do things
I will have to prove it to the king
When I am queen
I will be seen
I will be serene.

Eseosa Ogbe (8)
Mesne Lea Primary School, Worsley

My Deceased Dream

Once upon a time, long, long ago,
My mind contained an immense dream, and I shall tell you so,
I consisted of ambitious hopes - hopes that I wished to fulfil,
But the motive of war somehow managed to keep it still.

I was bred in Lebanon, with dreams of pursuing medicine,
I'd persist to save the vulnerable lives even when I'd have a wrinkled chin!
However hopeful I was, some things to man do not occur,
My dream wasn't possible 'til I'd be as dead as the rug's rabbit fur.

Another bomb, another airstrike was heard from my studious ears,
I had just commenced the medical test, then glared at the destruction in tears,
The loss of my brother was such a nightmare which no devoted could forget,
Now I wonder why rivalry was born, and life I now regret.

Yet I'm still robust, with my dreams in my eyes,
With care shall my brother look down,
At all the grades (that are fit for a doctor),
Which at the University of Beirut, I'd found.

My career is beside me, my dreams are fulfilled,
The life I have earned, I can see,
Oh, alas! I hear the whistle of an airstrike,
To the local shelter, I must flee!

A Continuation of the Reminiscences:
This is his sister writing, with sorrow and tears,
My two brothers: none could I save,
Now we sob before the posies,
Laid upon their graves.

It was I who wrote my brother's brief poem,
I read his diary soon,
He - the boy with obstacles in his path,
Had never managed to dance his tune.

Wafiq Chowdhury (11)
Mossford Green Primary School, Barkingside

My Voice Is A Noise!

My voice is loud,
It can travel through a crowd.
No time for discrimination
It can carry for a generation.
I can talk without a microphone,
I don't need to be quiet alone.

Sometimes when I use my normal voice,
People think I'm shouting and making a lot of noise.
I feel bad,
It's really sad.
People make mistakes and it is agreeable,
Like my voice needs to be acceptable.
Who does not make a mistake?
I want to see something as calm as a lake.

For once I thought I wasn't treated differently,
I accidentally thought of that, mistakenly.
Well, everything can change,
I guess it has to be strange.
Am I a ghost?
I think people don't like me the most.

All of those glorious days I liked,
Now tears I wiped.
You think it's hilarious,
I don't think that because I'm furious.
What if I treated you differently,
You'd go back crying to Italy.
At last, the discrimination has ended.
Not quite, it hasn't, I remembered.

Now I have a plan,
It smoothly began.
It now has been executed,
Can it succeed?
It's worth a try,
You can't deny!

My plan has succeeded,
Now I am highly treated.
Now I don't have any friends,
I'm trying something, it extremely depends.
It worked, now non-friend torture ends.
With my friend, I'm going on an Indian journey,
It's really worthy.

Maghizhini Manikandan (10)
Mossford Green Primary School, Barkingside

The Light Ahead Of Us

I close my eyes and go to sleep
But little did I know I entered a world of peace.
I wake up in the middle of nowhere,
And I see a magical world of extraordinaire.
Starlight fills my eyes,
As moonbeams rush by the skies.
What is this mysterious world I see?
Soaring like a bird in the open sky, I start breaking free.

As joy and jubilation fills the night,
I see stunning and fabulous fairies fleeing like a dove;
Flying and twirling around the ravishing rainbow in this world of love.
I realise I've entered a world of peace,
As beauteous winged horses start to release.
But in the distance, I see a light -
On this night, it glows bright.
I run over, desperate to see,
I get there and every creature crowds the golden sea.
"What does it symbolise?" I ask,
"I must know, I really must."
They tell me, "There is always a light ahead of us."

Aleena Choudhury (10)
Mossford Green Primary School, Barkingside

Pirate's Dream

In dreams, I sail the vast unknown,
Sailing swiftly on my ship named Bone,
The more quests I take,
The more I escape reality.
Now, I venture far, so listen with your ears,
This endless quest is one sure to bring tears.
So sit back tight as this story unfolds,
As I journey far into the North Pole.
The adventure was hard as my sword is sharp,
We sailed on the waves, eating plenty of carp,
We knew treasure awaited through the icy north.
With my hands on the helm and my eyes on the sea,
I knew my journey would end drinking a cup of tea.
"Land ho!" I shouted as we approached the shore.
With a map in our hand and our journey on foot,
The treasure it holds was sure to be found.
With the treasure just there out of arms reach,
My quest ends on the sandy beach.
So sail, mateys and seek treasure afar,
For stories untold is where true adventures are.

Elias Thawe (10)
Mossford Green Primary School, Barkingside

Space Dreams

My dream is to go to space,
To see meteorites, comets and asteroids race.
Cosmic colours fill my eyes,
While rainbow nebulas lie in the sky
Black holes could suck up the whole Earth!
There are stars up there, shining with mirth.
Billions of galaxies, perhaps even more,
But we are safe in the Milky Way, right at its core.
A prism of colours from auroras illuminate our nights,
And the moon reflects the sun's beams onto us, giving us light.
There are gas giants like Jupiter and Saturn,
And their icy neighbours; Uranus and Neptune.
These are the Jovian planets, much bigger than Earth and the moon.
Thousands of satellites orbit around Earth's surface
Protecting our planet from space objects lost.
Eight planets continue to twirl around our dwarf star, the sun,
And to think our discoveries of the Universe have only just begun.

Zaynab Ali (11)
Mossford Green Primary School, Barkingside

Land Of Dreams

In a land of magic and mystery,
Where dragons soar and wizards grieve.
The forest whispers secrets untold,
And knights seek adventures so bold.

Through ancient ruins and forgotten tombs,
Echoes of legends are heard in the gloom,
Sorcerers cast their spells with ease,
While fairies dance beneath moonlit trees,
A realm of wonder, a realm of dreams,
Where nothing is quite as it seems.

In this fantasy dream, reality fades,
And imagination weaves its intricate braids,
Where wishes are granted and heroes rise,
And every heart's desire takes to the skies.

So close your eyes and drift away,
To a world that you'll dream of every day.

Sanda Bargan (11)
Mossford Green Primary School, Barkingside

Floating In Space

In my dream, beyond our earthly bounds,
A whole new realm of wonder surrounds.
Infinite galaxies and moons,
A cosmic dance to the universe tunes.

Nebulas and blackholes, so vast and grand,
Mysteries, yet we have to understand,
Saturn's ring, Jupiter's great red spot,
Astronomical wonders that leaves us in awe.

May we continue to explore and learn,
And still let our imaginations forever burn,
Now I can say bravely and proud,
That dreaming is totally allowed.

Michelle Naing (10)
Mossford Green Primary School, Barkingside

A Good Day

In my dreams every night,
I fly to the clouds with might.
Today, the sun is in the air,
All the spiders are in their lair.
But now the fairies come out to play,
We can now start the day.
While the pixies skip around the bend,
Lunchtime is coming to an end.
The stars are twinkling in the sky,
So now it's time to say goodbye.

Amaiya Patel (10)
Mossford Green Primary School, Barkingside

My 'Fanta-Sea'

N ight was here and I was in my comfy bed. My head was resting on my fluffy pillow
I was now in a deep sleep. I looked around, however all I saw was the colourful coral and the fluorescent fish.
G oing deeper into the vibrant coral I saw an adorable axolotl and some peaceful pufferfish playing in the spectacular seaweed. It was all amazing!
H overing by was a hopeful horseshoe crab going to meet his friend, the adventurous axolotl to start their journey.
T hen the wondrous waves washed me to the sandy beach. I love how the sand felt brushing between my toes.
M y heart was bouncing, I was overjoyed. I ran through the wondrous waves admiring the scene around me.
A nd just like that I woke up and I realised waking up was the nightmare, as my 'Fanta-sea' was just a dream after all.
R ealising this made me feel disappointed and upset, however, I really had some wonderful memories and that's what matters.
E very little underwater animal was special to me in their own way.

Izzy Phipps (9)
Oldcastle Primary School, Bridgend

Once Upon A Dream

O nce, a little girl had a dream
N ia was her name, she had a dream she was in space
C hristmas was close, so Nia was writing her list, but she didn't want toys, she had a wish
E very night, Nia would look up and wish she was floating with the stars.

U pon the stars, Nia would be the brightest there
P rofessor, her dad, was a professor; for Christmas, he made her a rocket
O ne night, Nia heard weird noises from the garage
N ia read a lot about rockets, so she sat in the rocket and flew to space.

A nd Nia was in space! She got out and explored.

D ancing on the moon, Nia found aliens
R ays of sun were all she could see. She was waking up
E ventually, Nia got out of bed and went downstairs
A nd her mum and dad asked her what she dreamed about
"**M** aybe later," said Nia, "it's a long story."

Amelia Parfitt (8)
Oldcastle Primary School, Bridgend

My Fairy Dream

Fairies love luscious things,
But be careful of their tiny wings.
You may think their wings are strong,
But I believe that you are wrong.
Their wings are delicate, fine and thin,
But here is something about how they begin.
When a baby's first laugh floats away,
You will watch it land and say,
"What's that on the floor?
Nothing much, just a fairy, no more!"
Which I know you will love,
As much as a white dove.
They live in a magical house,
In the house, they have a pet mouse.
On top of the house, they have a cherry pot,
They also have a fairy cop,
A fairy teacher,
And a fair greeter.
They love to play,
And have fun all day.
So always leave out
A fairy house.

Eloise Jones (9)
Oldcastle Primary School, Bridgend

My Dream Giraffe

One evening, my family and I
Were sitting down to dinner
When, *ding-dong*, the doorbell rang
Can you guess who was at our door?

"Hello," said a curious voice from up high
But all I could see were legs from my height
Staring at me was the familiar face
Of Rice, the giraffe and his cute spotty smile

Rice, the giraffe, had escaped from the zoo
I dropped him from my pushchair when I was two!
Now he was back and larger than life
So, I asked him to tea, because I thought that was nice

Now, Rice and I are back as best friends
And we will be together until the end.
Unfortunately, my alarm rang, it was time to get up
It was nice to dream of Rice all grown up!

Hattie Lancett (9)
Oldcastle Primary School, Bridgend

My Friend Zed

When I go to bed at night,
I dream of all the stars so bright.
Today when I went to bed
I started to dream of my friend, Zed.
Me and Zed were on a spaceship
And we were heading to the moon!
Me and Zed were having fun
When Zed smelt something that made him go, "Yum!"
We decided to take a closer look
And we saw that the moon was made of cheese!
"Yippee, yippee!" We both yelled really crazy.
When we finally landed on the moon
Me and Zed felt brand new.
We played and played for hours on end
Until my friend woke me up.
So I said goodbye to Zed
And got up to make my bed.

Fara Docherty (9)
Oldcastle Primary School, Bridgend

Fantasy

F ish and sharks slowly meander through the dark and mysterious water.
A wave from the powerful ocean rises up, like an arm reaching for the glistening stars.
N ervous and cautious, deep and alone, the crazy chase begins.
T he temperature of the murky blue water drops like a stone.
A great white shark, with lightning speed, darts through the water like a bullet train.
S tartled and scared, I swim towards the light.
Y elling and crying all through the night, I suddenly wake with panic and fright.

Lottie Thomas (9)
Oldcastle Primary School, Bridgend

Friendship

F riends are gifts you can't live without,
R elying on each other without any doubt,
I look to the future and all I see,
E ndless good times, you and me,
N ear or far, I will always be here,
D ancing by your side, do not fear,
S haring moments together, some happy, some sad,
H oping one day we will look back at all the good times we've had,
I n the meantime, my friend, please stay by my side,
P laying together, come along for the ride!

Effie John (8)
Oldcastle Primary School, Bridgend

The Wishing Guitar

In my dreams, I'm in the sky,
I'm relaxing on a cloud, I don't know why
When I was there, I saw this star
And it gave me a wishing guitar
It said, "You can think of anything."
But nothing came to my head except a *ding*
I thought I could play a tune on the guitar
And it would be about the planet Mars
The star said quickly, "Wake up, it's nearly dawn!"
So I did and I woke up with a giant yawn.

Oona Taylor (9)
Oldcastle Primary School, Bridgend

Flying Fairies

F airies flying around in the air floating their wings and weaving their hair
A ll around the fairies sing and laugh in the lush green meadow
I n the forest, the fairies skip into their treehouse tower whilst dancing up their wooden staircase
R eading their rhyming fairytale stories in their cosy, warm beds
Y ounger fairies flew happily to the fun park and practised their flying trick from dawn 'til dusk.

Sofia Hearne (9)
Oldcastle Primary School, Bridgend

Nightmare! Acrostic!

N othing but joint suffering.
I n the dark, big world where happiness is a crime.
G hosts of my past are moving closer.
H issing and fighting in the wars of karma.
T orturing me while I have my nightmare.
M aking me breathe faster and faster.
A nd all I can hear is my heart beating.
R iding around my soul.
E very day I think about it!

Bette George (9)
Oldcastle Primary School, Bridgend

Olympic Gold

I am standing on the podium
My team is all around me
Gold medals dangling from our necks
The crowd is cheering loudly

They raise the flag up high
A Welsh dragon in the air
We wrap our arms around each other
A proud moment we all share

The anthem starts and we sing along
Tears of joy fall down my face
My dream of winning Olympic gold
Has finally taken place.

Heidi Baldwin (9)
Oldcastle Primary School, Bridgend

Dreaming

D rifting away to a magical place
R emembering dreams that have put a smile on your face
E ach dream is different in its own way
A ll dreams happen in the night, not the day
M emories of family and pets that we miss
I magining giving them a hug and a kiss
N ever forget dreams can come true
G oing to bed is an amazing time for you.

Maisy Leah Robinson (8)
Oldcastle Primary School, Bridgend

Squishmallow

S quishy and squashy
Q uick to flip
U nbelievably relaxing
I love to squeeze them
S quidgy and cwtchy
H appy and soft
M ulti-coloured galaxies
A world of fun!
L ove to play
L ots of cool colours and designs
O h, they are so cute and adorable
W ow, I love Squishmallows!

Gracie Rose Pring (8)
Oldcastle Primary School, Bridgend

Spiders Vs Violet

S piders crawling in my dreams
P rowling and prancing in groups of three
I ntimidating me, I wish they would flee
D isappearing under my bed, do they want to be fed?
E ight long legs, black and hairy, I wish they weren't so big and scary
R eaching for a glass to carry them away
S piders be gone, Dad saves the day!

Violet Powell (8)
Oldcastle Primary School, Bridgend

Blooming Blossoms

Big blossoms swaying in the wind
Just like the pretty roses bloom.
Daffodils, bluebells, snowdrops grow
And dance along the breeze.

A sprinkle of rain, a dash of sun
The flowers dance some more.
In my dreams, they grow and grow,
Then dance a little more.

Isla Evans (8)
Oldcastle Primary School, Bridgend

Flying Footballer And Stadium

F ootball, imagine it in space, well that's what happened today
L ions versus Bulls up in space, a flying football stadium
"Y eah!" That's what everyone says but I don't like that the Lions are losing
I n space, the Bulls are winning up high
N ervous Lions fans, we are going to draw probably, or maybe score I hope
G asping, the Lions get a penalty to equalise and they score!

F ans are going crazy!
O h Lions respect, they don't celebrate
O h fans are going off celebrating
T wo fans are screaming
B alls with Lions pictures are on the pitch
A ll Lions fans are jumping
L ife, we are on TV for life
L iving life we are celebrating
E lectric Lions' mood is cheering the Bulls fans up
R esult, we win!

Elliott Seeley (8)
Pheasey Park Farm Primary School, Great Barr

World Final Football Match

One day I saw a UFO,
The lights on it started to glow,
They challenged us to football and I said no,
But otherwise, they said the world would blow!

So we assembled the team of a dream,
I was the captain, this is my football team,
When we stepped on the pitch,
The team was a glitch,

The aliens were ready from space,
And as I tied up my lace,
We were shot into the sky,
With dragons flying by, we were really high,

The game was tied at two to two,
When I ran up to try and shoot,
As he steps in my way, he makes me fall,
Penalty awarded, the keeper stands big and tall.

Swoosh! As it hits the back of the net,
Leaving the goalie on the ground, wet,
The top corner is where it curled,
Now what is safe, is the world.

As the captain grabs the cup,
The whole team gets to lift it up,
At last, the world can keep on,
As my football team has shone.

Joshua Anderson (9)
Pheasey Park Farm Primary School, Great Barr

My Life Turned Upside Down

I was in my comfy bed,
Looking like a tired, sleepyhead.
I woke up and walked upon the sidewalk,
To see a crawling, slithering hawk, squawk!

I saw a monster walking the plank,
And a pirate in a miniature tank,
A tooth fairy breathing flaming fire,
And a dragon collecting teeth from under children's smelly pillows, by a dirty wire.

But then everybody was screaming, saying the candy queen was seen eating a bean,
And I think the candy queen was very keen,
Then the next thing I saw was dancing slugs,
And adorable tiny talking pugs.

Wait! I didn't wake up,
I was dreaming I saw a pup!
So cute, can you agree,
Oh no! I don't want to see the dog wee!

Bethany Fisher (9)
Pheasey Park Farm Primary School, Great Barr

Fredbear Peak

I'm sleeping peacefully in my bed,
But the ground's rumbling making me bob my head.
All of a sudden there is a *boom, bang, crash!*
People scream outside as I rush out.
"Is everything okay?" I say with a doubt.
I look up and then I see the eruption of Fredbear Peak!
Smoke and ash fill the air, when is the lava going to leak?

The ground gives a rumble as the thunder arrives,
"This is going to be ba-." *Boom! Bang! Crash!*
"Run!" I hear people say
As the lava spills all over the bay,
So I ran and ran to the escape boat.
"Goodbye, Fredbear Peak," I say as we escape into the vast ocean.

Harry Myatt (9)
Pheasey Park Farm Primary School, Great Barr

Wicked Nightmare World

When you want to sleep at night,
She has to get a little fright.
Boom! went a loud sound where she was,
She thought she was the cause.

She entered an enchanted forest,
And was immediately cursed and walked the slowest,
An evil pirate started to show,
She was sure he was a foe.

She was stuck in a horrible dream,
She really needed a helpful team.
A wicked wizard offered to help,
She disagreed and started to yelp.

"Please can you take me back?"
He agreed and gave her a sack,
She was happy as she started to gleam,
She was happy it was just a dream.

Hameedah Shaibu (9)
Pheasey Park Farm Primary School, Great Barr

Crazy Clowns

C razy clowns roam the land with their powers.
R acing sparks fly from their pot, such amazing powers.
A s I look around, I see more and more clowns coming my way.
Z ooming red noses fly straight past me.
Y et we have more to go.

C lowns are creepy and scary, so we can't be scared.
L ots and lots of clowns coming to me, or maybe not.
O kay, will they do something scary or creepy?
W hat will happen next?
N obody knows what they will do.
S oon, they might stop being creepy and be nice.

They might be coming after you...

Lily Rose Farley (9)
Pheasey Park Farm Primary School, Great Barr

Dreams

Hogwarts is where I want to be
There are magical wonders to see
I'm accepted
Not rejected
I'm so happy.

I'm going on a magical train
To learn lots of wonderful things in my brain
I've got an owl as rough as a towel
But he howls as loud as a crowd
He is a cheerful thing, but he bites
Be careful, so you can avoid a fight.

I've arrived just in time
To learn some magic spells
As soon as I get there, I hear some loud bells
I'm in the great potion classroom
I make a really loud *boom*
Now I'm on a sky-high broom.

Benjamin Hampshire (8)
Pheasey Park Farm Primary School, Great Barr

My Dream

My dream is to do horse jumping,
Galloping, cantering and bumping.
When it is time to go to the show,
My horse is rearing and ready, let's go, go, go!

When I'm on my horse
He wants to get to the course.
Always ready to go,
I always love the show!

The best thing about it is jumping the three-foot fence,
We never leave a single dent.
If we were to win the show,
We would be filled with cheer when we go.

If it wasn't a dream, my little strawberry roan,
I would have a stable at the back of my home.

Isla Titchen (8)
Pheasey Park Farm Primary School, Great Barr

Pirates

I go on a walk and I see waves splashing up and down
Oh, look, the pirates are in town
They come in their boats
They are fast
They come in a blast
It is very scary
They are really hairy
I am alone, looking at the maps on my phone
I am on the beautiful sandy beach, I am petrified
I go for a swim
I see a fin
Oh, look, the sand is talking
Oh, look, now it's walking
Pirates are in awe
They can't believe what they saw
They run away quickly and never come back
Thank goodness, I was going to hide in a sack.

Sienna Dunn (9)
Pheasey Park Farm Primary School, Great Barr

Never-Ending Nightmare

When it is a creepy night,
She had a little fright,
Whoosh! She enters a haunted village,
It was definitely a horrible image.

They are not allowed red,
Or they will be dead.
A new person came in,
And put a red flower in the bin.

She is stuck in the dream,
People started to be mean.
An evil wizard appeared,
She began to get frightened.

"Take me back, take me back!"
Boom! She woke up carrying a sack.
She thinks that is stressful,
But her brother found it wonderful!

Karis Chan (9)
Pheasey Park Farm Primary School, Great Barr

Dreams

If I was a princess,
My castle would be pink.
Pink turrets, pink bricks,
Pink indoor things,
That would make me wink.
If I was a princess,
A carriage I would ride,
The wheels spin,
The horses neigh,
It will never hide.
If I was a princess,
I would have a beautiful voice.
The whispers clear,
That everyone can hear,
This gorgeous, non-stop noise.
If I was a princess,
I would have a handsome prince.
He'd own a robin,
A red-ringed robin,
A prince had ever since.
Dream finished.

Niamh Guilfoyle (9)
Pheasey Park Farm Primary School, Great Barr

Extinction!

D oes nothing to be prepared for this epic moment waiting for me
I take a step, I've never been so nervous before
N o humans to be seen
O h, please be a dream, am I still fast asleep?
S een not by a human but a T-rex! Being followed
A round the corners I go as the night light shines
U nder I go to hear a blow-up above the trees and blind the T-rex
R un! I only have a few minutes to go!
S afe again in my home in my bed from that dreadful nightmare in my head!

Minnie McKeown (8)
Pheasey Park Farm Primary School, Great Barr

My Dream

S howjumping is my dream,
H ow do I stop daydreaming?
O ver some jumps, my horse and me, let's go!
W e could win as a team!
J umping over the course, trying not to look down,
U nder and over the poles and jumps, me and Stella go.
M aybe me and Stella could win! *Bang!* on the grass,
P eople all around me in my competition,
I 'm super close to winning a medal,
N early there, a chance, I can win!
G o, go! I have won the gold medal!

Bella-Louise Reynolds (8)
Pheasey Park Farm Primary School, Great Barr

Planets And Universe

In space, you can see the stars and Mars,
Space is like a race, so run as fast as a blast,
When you're on the moon
You can see its mighty booming glow,
The sky is black as the night,
It is a beautiful sight.
Galaxies, universes and the stars,
I wonder what life would be like on Mars,
As I wonder this,
The thoughts and surroundings become bliss,
Rockets hiss,
I blow my family one big kiss.
I wonder what life is like back home.
I wish upon a star that I could call on my phone.

Erica Melintescu (8)
Pheasey Park Farm Primary School, Great Barr

Wizarding World

Magic whispering everywhere,
Some even going through your hair,
Spells and potions to be done,
That sounds amazing and also fun!

Broomsticks fly up in the sky,
Some people eating a nice hot pie,
Dragons breathing fire, now *boom! Kick! Pow!*
Witches showing off, wow, just wow!

Books flying from shelf to shelf,
But what they're chasing, yourself.

I hope you like my wizarding world,
But let me tell you, it is very cold!

Seren Thomas (9)
Pheasey Park Farm Primary School, Great Barr

The Vet Paradise

The vets is a wonderful place to be,
There are lots of beautiful animals to see,
Except for when your beloved friend,
Unfortunately passes away.
It is the saddest kind of day.
Ding! Suddenly a patient
Walks in with a frog,
As muddy as a bog,
A dog comes in,
As sore as a boar.
Animals are waiting to be checked.
The queues are long,
The animal howls are a song.
I can't wait anymore,
My dog is letting out a loud, big snore!

Eva Barclay (9)
Pheasey Park Farm Primary School, Great Barr

Magical Land

Far away in the distance,
A magical world was created,
Me and my friend were really curious and went on an adventure,
We look around,
And saw sprinkles on the ground,
We saw a fairy,
Her name was Mary,
There were lots of sweets,
It is such a treat,
On the land there were lots of treats and candy,
One of the candies was talking, she was called Sandy,
There was love and sweetness in the air,
It has too much love and sweet air, it blows my hair.

Josette Yue (9)
Pheasey Park Farm Primary School, Great Barr

Once Upon A Dream

Once upon a dream,
My heart beams.

At night, I curl up in my bed,
A carnival swirls around my head,
Fast rides and tasty treats,
But there's one thing that makes my heart beat,
There's a clown, he suddenly sees me,
He's chasing me, I can't get free,
I circle round rides to make him dizzy,
He won't stop running, he won't let me be, it's crazy,
I don't think I will ever be able to get out of here!

Evie-Rose Barrowclift (9)
Pheasey Park Farm Primary School, Great Barr

In The Sky

Up in the sky,
Beaming as I fly,
Flying all on my own,
Whilst talking on the phone,
White, soft clouds,
Whirring above the grounds,
As I happily and calmly lift,
Below me, I see a long drift,
As I fly, lonely,
While other people play happily,
Soaring through the air,
As you look down, you will see a fair,
Keep flying and flying and dreaming,
As people are snoring in their beds,
Resting their sleepy little heads.

Victoria Saskowska (9)
Pheasey Park Farm Primary School, Great Barr

Flying High

F lying while lying in the air nobody will ever dare
L ight in the night
Y ellow lights shining bright getting closer tonight
I ce cold air I had a bad dare while in the air
N ow in the air we fly fine
G ulp, there goes the doors

H igh in the true-blue sky
I ce falling all around, burr! It is cold
G o, let's go out the back door
H elp, I'm flying away, catch me!

Toby Boekbinder (9)
Pheasey Park Farm Primary School, Great Barr

Once Upon A Dream

Of all the magical lands
Where the fairies will fly,
There are dragons and clowns wandering around.
You might be a teacher or a builder,
But down, down below
There are monsters to see,
With spiders all under the sea.
Now you'll fall into endless darkness
Where the monsters roam,
And find the fear to make you heartless
But remember it's just a dream.
For all of the scary nights
That carry all of the frights.

Sofia Chen (9)
Pheasey Park Farm Primary School, Great Barr

Forest Animals

Meow, meow, there was a cat,
That sat on my hat.

Woof, woof, there was a dog,
That sat on a log.

Neigh, neigh, there was a horse,
That gallops over the course.

Oink, oink, there was a pig,
It was running around wearing a wig.

Cluck, cluck, there was a chicken,
It was licking.

Moo, moo, there was a cow,
The cow wants milk now.

Erin Summlar (9)
Pheasey Park Farm Primary School, Great Barr

Superstar!

S uddenly I see blue smoke making me cough out loud,
U p I jump with people looking proud,
P laying around are tiny unicorns! Wow!
E veryone is staring right now,
R eally? Is that a Galaxy bar? They're not out yet!
S o please do not fret!
T he sun is shaped like Oreo? *Whoosh!* What was that?
A hhh I am falling, *thud!*
R eally I was just dreaming!

Isabelle Taylor-Brown (9)
Pheasey Park Farm Primary School, Great Barr

Football

F orever I have dreamed of going inside a football stadium
O n my birthday. It has been my dream come true.
O n April fourth I am going to a stadium to watch a game.
T he time is nearly up and they're losing, one-nil.
B all's moving fast, scoring goal by goal
A t fifteen miles per hour, shooting down the pitch.
L ast minute: they score a goal and they score their
L ast goal.

Harvey Wilde (8)
Pheasey Park Farm Primary School, Great Barr

Monster

M illions of people are scared of me, with claws
O n my hands and with my teeth as sharp as knives
N o one can walk without shaking in fear when they
S ee me going down the street. You would let out a loud screech
T he people all scream at me, so I have no friends. I see monsters
E verywhere. Big ones, small ones, purple ones, black ones
R oaring is all you can hear for miles and miles.

Juliette Boreham (8)
Pheasey Park Farm Primary School, Great Barr

The World Cup

W in, screamed the fans of England
O n the day of the final, Argentina wins
R unning down the line is Kylian Mbappé
L ionel Messi passes back to Di Maria... *Goal!*
D enmark concedes a goal and loses.

C asemiro shoots, but Jordan Pickford saves it
U raguay score a goal in the twentieth minute
P anama concedes goal after goal, there is no hope!

Riley Lander (9)
Pheasey Park Farm Primary School, Great Barr

Magic Lands

There's cotton candy, it's so sweet,
There are lots of treats,
My cotton candy's name
Is Sandy.

I saw a fairy,
It was a little hairy,
It was magic,
A bird cried, it was tragic.

Plop, there's a ring on my hand,
The explosion is going *bang* like a band,
Argh! A witch,
My computer had a glitch,
There's a hole,
I scored a goal.

Simreet Kaur (9)
Pheasey Park Farm Primary School, Great Barr

They Day I Went To Villa Park

F ootball is known as a worldwide sport
O nly one person is known as the GOAT (Greatest Of All Time)
O ne team wins the Premier League
T he shot gets fired at the goal
B *ang, crash*
A ll the people can't believe what they saw
L ots of record-breaking goals for you and me
L oyal fans watch the breathtaking match and can't wait to go back.

Benjamin Wacogne (8)
Pheasey Park Farm Primary School, Great Barr

Nightmares

N ight is when I sleep,
I start to have dreams,
G oing to the woods and getting lost,
H aving to go to a scary house with a monster, a clown and a doll,
T hen I got to sleep in a scary place,
M orning comes,
A nd I forgot all about,
R evolting dreams and,
E vil scenes,
S cary nights are the worst.

Chikamdinaka Ugochukwu (8)
Pheasey Park Farm Primary School, Great Barr

In My Dreams

Once upon a dream,
Wait, I think I heard someone scream,
Lovely things in my head,
I don't even need to leave my bed.

Dinos in my sleep,
I can't even take a little peep,
They are roaring,
But snoring.

In my dream, I got dizzy,
But then I drank something fizzy,
In my dreams, anything can be,
Almost anything I can see.

Arun Kumar-Ford (9)
Pheasey Park Farm Primary School, Great Barr

Dream

In my bed, tucked up warm and tight,
I dreamt about a delightful dream last night,
With wonderful elephants flying,
Do you really think I'm lying?
And lovely, fluttering, magical fairies,
Eating lots of yummy berries,
And with glistening trees,
All around the beautiful seas,
Riding magical unicorns,
While admiring their glowing horns.

Lillie O'neill (9)
Pheasey Park Farm Primary School, Great Barr

Lost In The Wood!

When I look around,
I see the ground,
In the dark, gloomy trees,
It is such a breeze.
With Frey and Emilia by my side,
I hope we get a ride,
Then I see a book,
And I have a look,
The book is empty,
Then the book left me.
The forest is where I don't want to be,
I need to go home,
To go and get my phone.

Aria Law (8)
Pheasey Park Farm Primary School, Great Barr

Dreams

As I was sleeping, all snug and tight
I dreamt about royalty all night.

They ruled over England happily
We all praised them merrily.

They went about their duties with a smile on their face
Especially Princess Catherine, who was full of grace.

I wished I could be King for a day
Doing all duties, home and away.

Jay Smith (8)
Pheasey Park Farm Primary School, Great Barr

The Acrostic Ball

F ear of football is not to be afraid,
O ops, I missed, get me under the shade.
O h, go on, have a shot.
T hen get me some pots.
B e kind at the end of the match,
A nd be careful, there might be a patch.
L earn games to play good.
L earn kids, yes you should.

Elliott Anderson (8)
Pheasey Park Farm Primary School, Great Barr

All About Football At Villa Park

As I looked around
I had happiness
Inside my heart
I had a feeling
That I'm going
To enjoy it
I'm really excited
What is inside
In Villa Park?
When I went inside
I was shocked to see
What was inside
Of Villa Park for me
I really hope I can
Visit again.

Addison Webb (8)
Pheasey Park Farm Primary School, Great Barr

Arcade

Walking in, I hear a sound
Coming from the punching pound
When I got there, it was shaking like never before
I go to the toilet, and there is more
Then I punched it like slamming a door.

Then a person jumps out onto the floor
He was punching again, and it was a pain
It felt like a cane.

Ted Seeley (8)
Pheasey Park Farm Primary School, Great Barr

Dreams

Once upon a dream, I see lots of steam
Out it comes from a magical train
So much magic to fill my brain
Hogwarts is where I want to be
There's no other place I want to see
I learn to fly on my broom
Make potions in every room
There is magic all around me
Here is where I feel free.

Paige Johnson (8)
Pheasey Park Farm Primary School, Great Barr

Dreams

What a beautiful place with fairies dancing
And magical, colourful unicorns prancing.
The clock is ticking through the night,
This dream is such a delight.
It's a place I always love to be,
A place where I always feel free.
Beautiful rainbows fill the sky,
In my dreams, I can fly.

Thea Hadgkiss (8)
Pheasey Park Farm Primary School, Great Barr

Dreams

My football team is like a dream
Soon, we will be riding down the stream
I go to sleep
And I hear a bleep
And I dream about the World Cup
I woke up. I was playing a football match
Everyone was shouting my name
There were goals shooting in every hole
"We win!" I got a flying trophy, it said 'Goal'!

Amelia Forrester (8)
Pheasey Park Farm Primary School, Great Barr

Footy Kicks

Back at the pitch,
The fantastic magic ball does a glitch.
It makes me as tall as a giraffe,
While my belly starts to laugh,
The ball is so magic,
It makes my skills less tragic,
I can do forty kicks,
When my manager picks
The man of the match,
I'm always the catch.

Dylan Bhopla (9)
Pheasey Park Farm Primary School, Great Barr

Animal Poem

Tiger Tim roars!
He's the biggest tiger I ever saw,

The snake slithers slowly,
He watches very closely,

There was a fish
That has a big wish,

There was a lion,
His name was Dion,

Parrot squawks in the trees,
He does not like a bee.

Serenity Bartholomew (8)
Pheasey Park Farm Primary School, Great Barr

Dreams

In my bed, all tucked up tight
I had an amazing dream last night
I was a pirate, mighty and brave
Searching for treasure in every cave
Plenty of bottles filled with rum
Oh, how I love to fill my tum
Careful, I'll make you walk the plank
Where many other prisoners sank!

Olivia Bland (9)
Pheasey Park Farm Primary School, Great Barr

My Dream World

I love living in my mansion
But it was an expansion.

I was in my bed at night
But then I had a fight
I had a great dream
That I was on a beam.

I was kicking a ball
Because I was tall
I was kicking for a goal
But I hit a pole.

Esmae Hollyhead (8)
Pheasey Park Farm Primary School, Great Barr

Dream

When I'm in my dream, I see a ship
Pirates going on a trip
They're always on a hunt for treasure
This gives them great pleasure
When I go deep down in the sea
A Kraken is in front of me
It's a fight to survive
I need to stay alive.

Drew Wheller-Grice (8)
Pheasey Park Farm Primary School, Great Barr

Dreams

I dream of a magical place
I can't wipe the smile off my face
Hogwarts is where I want to be
Magic spells are waiting for me
I learn to fly on a broom
Make potions in every room
Hogwarts is my happy place
Permanent smile on my face.

Mikaeel Puri (8)
Pheasey Park Farm Primary School, Great Barr

Dream

In my bed, all tucked up tight,
As I had a delightful dream last night.
I thought of pirates in my dream,
They were going to make me walk the beam
I was searching for treasure; look how it is so big and bright,
It awoke me last night.

Ella-Rose Darby (8)
Pheasey Park Farm Primary School, Great Barr

Dreams

The fish came by me
We sat down by the sea.

I saw a sparkling shell and its pearl,
And saw a big crab with another crab, it's a girl.

Let's make a cannon spark,
To scare away the sharks.

Hafee Siddiqui (9)
Pheasey Park Farm Primary School, Great Barr

Dancer In The Hall

D eep, tall hall
A nd long, blonde hair
N ice new clothes and
C olourful leotards
E veryone dances amazingly
R outines and bright lights

I love being a dancer.

Olivia-Rae Byrne (8)
Pheasey Park Farm Primary School, Great Barr

Dream

A boy was in space,
With a smile on his face,
He was walking on the moon,
All around, he did zoom.

Alfie Heath (9)
Pheasey Park Farm Primary School, Great Barr

Dream Team

When I curl up in my bed,
Dreams of football fill my head.
Tonight I'm on the England team,
The fans around me shout and scream.
The stadium's full, us girls are ready,
The whistle has blown, keep calm and steady.
Keira Walsh has got the ball,
She passed but Alessia Russo falls.
The opposition is looking strong,
But I'm on a roll and I can't go wrong.
Round one player, then the next,
The goalie gets ready, her muscles flexed.
I run and run, I see the goal,
I have a burning deep inside my soul.
I use my skills, my power and passion.
I strike the ball in a perfect fashion.
I look at the goalie, and give her a glare,
I control the ball and kick it into the air.
It hits the net, she doesn't have a chance,
I run to the corner flag and do a little dance.

Cassie Desborough (9)
Potton Primary School, Potton

My Magical Lands

My magical lands are full of glee,
Where yellow flowers grow on trees.

Darting across the purple grass,
Rainbow-coloured stripy giraffes.

Dancing around in the light of the moon,
Are crazy orange bright baboons.

Can you hear it?
Chomp! Chomp! Chomp!
It's the sound of the crocs in the marshmallow swamp.

What's that over there?
It's a big, red, giant hare!

All the creatures huddle together,
For such a long time, it seems like forever.

I wonder what they're talking about,
I hope it's something I won't doubt,

They turn around and tell me to join in,
Because it's time to celebrate their win,

They tell me they won a competition,
To be the best town in the kingdom,

We dance all night,
Till our eyes shut tight,

Then, I say my goodbyes,
And they say, "See you next time."

A second later, I find myself in bed,
With wonderful thoughts stuck in my head.

Emilia Phillips (9)
Potton Primary School, Potton

When I Went To Bed Last Night

When I went to bed last night,
I dreamt of bunnies leaping in delight.
I dreamt of flowers starting to bloom.
I dreamt of wolves howling at the moon.
There were fireflies, lighting up the trees.
I saw them dancing beneath my knees.

I felt the calming breeze blowing past my face,
My heart was thumping. It began to race.
And, as I stared up at the stars
I spotted, in the distance, the planet Mars.
Just then, I spotted a green glow.
It got closer and closer. It was now very low.

It was strange. It was bright.
My eyes were blinded by the beaming light.
And out popped an alien, as weird as can be.
It smiled and it said, "Come and dance with me."
So we danced and we pranced. We did this until sunrise.
And, in the end, I woke up and opened my sleepy eyes.

Amber Schultz (9)
Potton Primary School, Potton

In The World Of Candy

In the world of candy,
Lived a boy called Andy.
He was very kind,
Candy canes he did not mind.
Sherbet lemons and lollipops,
Strawberry laces and rainbow drops.
Chocolate and Haribos,
Nothing like Jalapenos.
In the world of candy,
Lived a boy called Sandy.
He wasn't selfish,
Though he did like Swedish fish.
Chocolate was his fave,
He practically lived in a candy cave!
In the world of candy,
Lived a girl called Mandy.
She really wasn't mean,
Her favourite was a cherry jelly bean.

That's what's in the world of candy.

Aina Roberts (8)
Potton Primary School, Potton

My Journey To Slumberland

My room began to sparkle
My teddy jumped to life
I began to rise
Realising my bed could fly.

We flew high in the sky
Across mountains and seas
Was this really a dream?
It was the most beautiful thing I'd ever seen.

A dark smoke arose
Appearing to swallow everything
Its arrival was frightening
It was the Nightmare King.

I hopped off my bed
Standing tall and proud
This was the Nightmare King
And he wasn't messing around.

This was my dream
This was my fantasy
And the Nightmare King's presence
Faded right in front of me.

I awoke, lying in bed
Looking around, I shook my head
Silly me, I thought
It was just a dream.

Akorede West (8)
Potton Primary School, Potton

The Wonder Mystery!

Once upon a time
There was Ron, Fin, Nena
They were going on a magical adventure
Nena packed the stuff
While there were concentrating people
And she made everyone angry.

When everyone left
They followed the map to a castle
"Is this the right place?" said Nena.
"Yes!" said Ron.
"Let's go in!" exclaimed Fin.
When they came in the magic castle
They were glued to the magic wand
They all touched it
It was magical
From the majestic couple...!

Ellie Elias (9)
Potton Primary School, Potton

Amazing Dinos And Unicorns

D ancing along with the dinosaurs
I n the wind and rain
N o frowns or grumbles in sight
O nly smiles and laughter

U ntil the unicorns arrive
N ow we have dinos and unicorns
I n the wild together
C ome on guys it's a party
O nly smiles allowed
R eady, set, go!
N ow let's party, dino unicorns.

Kayla Garrett (8)
Potton Primary School, Potton

When I Grow Up I Want To Become A Scientist

When I grow up I want to become a scientist
Because I like motions and lotions and mixtures of potions
I want to discover the world, using telescopes and microscopes, so I can make it a better place to live in
I get excited with occasional explosions
Physics or chemistry, biology or neurology?
I'm not quite sure which scientist I want to become yet
What do you want to be?

Sakina Duggal (9)
Potton Primary School, Potton

Edna Mole

Edna Mole lived in a hole
With her pet mole
And she liked making inventions, at least that was her goal
But the most bizarre thing was her pet mole
Liked drinking juice from a bowl!
He said it was good for the soul
But good old Edna invented a drinking bowl
She called it a mole bowl
And it was a magic refilling bowl
Good old Edna Mole.

Ava-Mai McCarthy (8)
Potton Primary School, Potton

Teacher

T he teacher is teaching the class
E verything is spooky
A round me is horrifying
C an I save the day?
H elp, I'm lost, I don't know what to do
E veryone, where are you?
R ound the area it's a wolf, run!

Brooklynn Donegan (8)
Potton Primary School, Potton

Football

Football was my dream
On tall blades of grass
There would be a good team
Ball to ball, pass to pass
A good striker would do the trick
A striker that would be nice and quick
Football is my dream
I wish I had a decent team.

Nathan Cornwall (9)
Potton Primary School, Potton

My Weird Cat Dream!

There's one thing that I love the most, my cat!
She's the best cat ever!
But tonight I can't find her.
Poof! Whoosh! Bang!
I felt like I was falling...
Then I landed *boom!*
I was in a room
Full of cats!
They were singing
La, la, la, la!
I ran around looking for my cat
There were soft ones, fluffy ones, fat ones and nippy ones!
I climbed up walls and when I found my cat I hugged her
Whoosh! Poof! Bang!
I was back, my cat was as well
Looking as ginger as gingerbread.

Emily Platt (8)
Sunninghill Preparatory School, South Walks

The House Of Sweets

The kitchen is made of dripping chocolate
The house is decorated with M&Ms as colourful as a rainbow
Inside, wow a big family of pretty gumdrops
The walls are made of the tastiest gingerbread
The clouds are made of candyfloss
The door is made of the sweetest fudge
Chocolate buttons cover the rooftops
A river of Smarties outside the house
The doorknob is marked with an S for sweeties.

Sonny Hamlin (8)
Sunninghill Preparatory School, South Walks

The Sweetie Village

In the Sweetie Village
The trees are lollipops
They dance every night
Bushes are cupcakes
Houses are hard chocolate
Made by hand
Toilets are made of M&Ms
Yum, yum, yum!
Boom! You start to get hungry
Go to the Caramel Hotel
Last but not least, the sweet shop!
It is as edible as a tomato.

Freya Holland (7)
Sunninghill Preparatory School, South Walks

The Lego School

Our school is made of Lego!
Every time we open a door it breaks
When you jump the floor shakes
Then it recreates
In the air, we look at each other's hair
Our chairs are made out of squares
But a bear came into school and broke the hall.

William Kerr (7)
Sunninghill Preparatory School, South Walks

Baby Tigers

Baby tigers are so cute
They wear tiny little boots
They are as stripey as a zebra
And they run fast, *whoosh*
They read tiny little books
They have wings that fly up to the sky
And they eat cheese from the moon.

Alice Wright (8)
Sunninghill Preparatory School, South Walks

Dreams

D irt bikes are as orange as a satsuma
R emember this poem is getting weird
E lectric cars sound like a spaceship
A pples are red and so crunchy
M ummies are wrapped in a tomb
S cream.

Beauden Mudge (7)
Sunninghill Preparatory School, South Walks

Wish Upon A Dream

D ance in the wind
R oar goes the wind
E ek goes the excited child
A h ah ah goes the dream
M y mummy quivers in excitement.

Daisy Baker (8)
Sunninghill Preparatory School, South Walks

In My Cosmic Dreams...

I soared, journeyed through the cosmic world of space,
In the home of stars, it was a luminous place.
Faster and faster I went, as rapid as a race car,
Faster I went, as speedy as a shooting star.
Oh no! Through the sky I rapidly and crazily whirled,
Crash! Bang! I crashed down on a vibrant world.
I was petrified because all I could find,
Was a bunch of colourful aliens with no colour inside.
On this planet I was frightened and alone with no help,
But suddenly I heard a young helpless girl start to yelp.
She was with an evil alien as scary as can be,
On his body, darkness was all to see.
His eyes were turquoise gems in the sun,
And his claws were blood-red stems, ready to run.
I clutched the little girl by the wrist,
And we plummeted away in a twist.
We jumped into a celestial UFO and went *whoosh!* into cosmic space,
And we soared away to a distant place.
I awoke in bed, about to scream,
But then I spluttered, oh it was all a dream!

Lily Atkinson (9)
Wath C Of E Primary School, Rotherham

What If Nightmares Were Real?

I awaken from my dream and what do I see?
A vampire's lair, as vast as a bear.
Meow! went the cats surrounding me
In the vampire's creepy lair, wearing a creepy stare.
Alone with the vampires and creepy cats
Everywhere like an army.
Bang! Bloodthirsty vampires erupted a volcano that was sleeping
Glancing left, glancing right, all I can see is smoke in sight.
Within seconds like a cheetah, I find myself pushing into the cage
Meanwhile, blood is filling my metal cage
Like a pool filling up.
Why? Will I die? Why me?
A manic grin spreads across the vampire's repulsive face
Leaving me wandering across my brain.
Knock, knock! Who could that be? Who could I see? Minions!
Minions running left and right, up and down. I can't even count!

I sobbed for a second while the blood was swimming in my cage.
Would the Minions help? Yes! Minions vs. Vampires
Vampires running and unfolding their mind
While Minions are glancing, showing bravery in sight.
Boom! The vampires screaming that they're scared
So the Minions win fair and square!
Minions grab the key with delight
Like a picture of a smiley face.

But was it all a dream?

Isobel Foley (10)
Wath C Of E Primary School, Rotherham

My House

Every night I have a fright
It's not a delight like strawberries and ice cream
It's deeper and creepier than that
It's a monster, not fairies, unicorns, monsters!
Very scary ones every night they come into my house
I don't know when or why, but they come
I cry very quietly at night, but somehow despite no noise, they can still hear me
I always close my eyes to go back to real life
Slam, goes my door when they break in
It's like their land is called Nightmares

N - comes at night to give me a fright
I see you at night
G lancing from left to right
H ow did they get there?
T *hud* when moving around
M y worst fear
A manic grin goes across their faces
R unning away at night
E erie eyes glowing in the moonlight
S uffering when they are around

Every night I wish I would have a dream
Not a horrid nightmare.

Alice Ashley (10)
Wath C Of E Primary School, Rotherham

Kids Rule The World

In the city streets, kids litter the world with candyfloss and cake
Where kids make the fun run wild
They sent joy through the vent
Squash the hate with a coconut wash with a tropical popsicle with a cola nut taste
Catch a coconut it'll be a delight
The stars dance with a lovely melody at night
Where they gleam a human sheep in their dream
A lake of lemonade is a beautiful delight
A fun where there's no end
Joy has no boundaries in a world where fun is unstoppable
Kids have no boundaries because there's no stop to joy and fun
At even a sugary week no end to anything not even a sugary treat
The runaway smell never stops it softly drifts into a state of delight
Sweets and chocolate all over, cakes and buns make the fun start to appear
Bounce on the trampolines and onto piles of sugary delight.

Riley Fitzgerald (10)
Wath C Of E Primary School, Rotherham

What If Avocados And Coconuts Took Over The World?

Could you imagine if avocados took over the world,
Alongside coconuts, they're just edible, right?
Why would they decide to try and put up a fight?
As that would be such a big, big fright.
They would take over the world in the middle of the night,
When you're tucked up in bed,
Talking to your uncle Fred.
Until you go for a midnight snack and you don't realise,
But pick up an avocado and you go ballistic with fear.
This is where avocados tickle the tail of your dog,
Till you let out a wail and even the people in jail.
But thankfully this all happened on a guacamole night,
As a green revolution took over the world,
Until they hustled in green delight.
They made a tasty dessert.
However there is still a green, green treat,
In a world where fun definitely had an annoying ending.

Harry Kittle (10)
Wath C Of E Primary School, Rotherham

Planets Made Out Of Food

Dreams can be anything
Dreams are made by your imagination
Dreams, dreams, how wonderful they are.

In my dreams every night
Planets dance around the moon
When it gets to noon, the planets fade for the sun to shine
Every time you dine, these planets appear so tiny so small
Like a star in the sky
When you see them you will fly in your dreams
Whoosh past us like an aeroplane
When you see them your brain will pop
The food will drop while the moon dances in the night sky
As you pass you might try to eat them
But the sky flies them back to whence they came
The moon shines while all the planets dance around in a circle
Every night just the same
As spaceships land, the sun shines in delight
People think they are stars but in fact
They are suns and planets.

Maisie Lloyd (9)
Wath C Of E Primary School, Rotherham

Cheeseland

I awaken from my deep sleep
I jump as my friend gives me the creeps
We walk out the door, ready for more
As today's adventure begins
I glance around, confused and then I feel amused
All around me is cheese, I look and feel pleased
My friend picks up the football and stands up tall
And breathes in
We walk to the park
I trip on tree bark and fall into a cheese person
I ask his name, and he asks the same
I reply, "Josh"
He says, "Cheesedude"
I exclaim, "Really!" not meaning to be rude
We ask him to play, he shouts, "Yay!"
The ball rolls into the lake
It's my friend's mistake
I jump in
I begin to sink
I realise it's quick cheese.

Josh Chandler (10)
Wath C Of E Primary School, Rotherham

A Dragon's Cave

I was with some friends adventuring a lake,
Until we came across a waterfall.
This wasn't an ordinary one though,
A mysterious cave lay behind.
We were curious so we ventured to explore and find,
Diamonds and gems were scattered around,
Roar! A mysterious dragon lived here,
Eyes as white and blank as pearl and snow,
With aqua-blue scales that were waterproof and fins for ears.
The dragon roared once again echoing across the cave
Thinking we would steal
Soon, it realised we wanted a ride
It taught us how to fly on its back.
The dragon said it had a family at sea,
They were separated as this dragon was a freshwater creature,
While the rest had a saltwater feature.

Poppy Edwards-Ratcliffe (10)
Wath C Of E Primary School, Rotherham

The Open World!

It all starts when three boys called Charlie, Harley and Jacob want to go into space,
They hadn't gone yet,
But it all changed after one perfect dream,
They pay £1 each to go on a bus which can take you to space,
When they got there they jumped off the bus,
They bumped into an alien with bright blue-green eyes, eight legs and no mouth,
It had teeth though,
The alien took them to eight different places,
These were Mercury, Venus, Earth, Mars, Jupiter, Saturn, Neptune and Pluto,
On the way back they stopped on the moon,
It looked like a big ball of cheese,
It was time to go back home on a giant meatball to Planet Zoogaba where they all could eat.

Charlie Hickling (9)
Wath C Of E Primary School, Rotherham

The Little Crow Who Lives In A Tree

I woke up and I was in a forest alone
I was nowhere near the place I call home
I'm lost
I can't see anything but dead trees
I find some keys
In a tree, I find a door
It wasn't colourful anymore
Unlocking the door, I hear a crow
That says a welcoming hello
Its wings are like a soft blanket
Eyes meeting mine with a kind glow
I look down at his feet below
They are like prickly spikes
All of a sudden he says, "I'll help you,
I will show you the way to go"
He swoops me up out of the tree
"I'm free!" I scream with glee
Before I go I must say bye
To the little crow up in the sky.

Viviana Exton (10)
Wath C Of E Primary School, Rotherham

Aliens Take Over

In my dream late at night,
I always fly through the rainbow light; *whoosh!*
I seem to land on a planet as see-through as ghosts
called Kepler-22B.
Interesting turquoise aliens with one eye are all I see,
Some are wearing vibrant, emerald shorts,
While others are naked, trying not to get caught...
One by one, they pass me by, tipper-tapper,
In the picturesque sky,
After a while, they stop for an hour,
And all I can think about is whether or not they'll devour...
When I'm not expecting it, they charge at me, *bang!*
All I see is their eyes, as white as paper, glaring at me...

Grace Foley (10)
Wath C Of E Primary School, Rotherham

To Be A Cat

I am in my bed,
When something hits my head.
I wake up, feeling small and furry,
And everything feels very blurry.
I've got paws that are dark and tiny,
Oh, I feel so lively!
I look up at the starlit sky,
And see something run by.
I climb out of the window,
Landing as softly as a pillow.
I smell a mouse,
And I look at my house.
Running through the street,
I hear my heart beat.
Excitement flows through me,
As I climb a tree.
A shooting star flies by,
Wow, it's so, so high!
I climb down happily,
But, suddenly, I run rapidly.
It's a dog!

Ellie Needham (10)
Wath C Of E Primary School, Rotherham

Finding A Yeti

In the mountains I will seek,
For a furry Yeti, white and bleak.
Search up high, search down low,
I need to find one, go, go, go.
While I'm running I look at the stars,
I even manage to see Mars.
One by one they pass me by,
Sparkling and twirling in the midnight sky.
Then I see one - a Yeti for real!
And I think to myself, this is so surreal!
I lead him into a cave, losing my mind,
I just want to tell everyone about my amazing find.
I bring him to my house,
And I feed him a fresh mouse.
Later I find out that he is a she,
And we become friends, my Yeti and me.

Reuben Hatton (10)
Wath C Of E Primary School, Rotherham

Nightmares

N othing has prepared me for this dream.
I step foot into my parents' room at 3am sharp.
G oodness, they are wrapped in deadly tarantula webs like mummies.
H igh up on the ceiling, the spiders lurk
T all legs skyscraping around the walls.
M y, how can I escape this madness?
A re they going to kill me in my own house?
R unning to the front door to see my dog eaten alive.
E erie eyes glow in the darkness, walls like the Devil's canvas.
S uddenly, I wake up to see my family safe and comfy in bed.

Ruby Heppenstall (9)
Wath C Of E Primary School, Rotherham

Once Upon A Dream

In my dreams every night,
People live in camouflaged mac 'n' cheese houses
All over the Solar System
With lava as ceilings, red sauce.
Up above there are friends, pets, animals
Monsters, dragons, pirates.
Dinos, aliens and clowns.
An adventure awaits.
Cold, happy dreams
Wait to be opened by your mind.
Even if the starlight goes
There's always a might with the light.
On Earth it's rare over there
With bear and despair.
When you wake up you see
That you're where you belong,
But it's all gone.

Jacob White (9)
Wath C Of E Primary School, Rotherham

Dreams

In my dreams every night
Unicorns gather around me with cotton candy clouds
Telling me to eat it and it tastes like the best cotton candy
But then my dream turned around
And the cotton candy turned into a monster
And I got frightened
It was as big as the BFG
I hid straight under my bed
But then all of a sudden
The unicorn turned into a big banana
Then everyone was giggling like we were in Heaven
Then it did it again
The banana unicorn's friend turned into a toilet
Everyone was laughing so hard they nearly lost their voice!

Effie Luana Murphy (9)
Wath C Of E Primary School, Rotherham

Monster Woods

In this place, all I can see
Are many trees and monkeys having wees
But deeper inside
You might even die
Because now the monsters are free
Not many people get out
You'll be living on sprouts
About as slow as a turtle
You've probably gone over a hurdle
The monsters are awake
They start an earthquake
You're next to a foe; it says, "Oh."
You run away
He looks at your face
You found a bunker
The monster has now sunken
But don't celebrate now
Because you're about to say oww.

Oliver Bankes (9)
Wath C Of E Primary School, Rotherham

Dreams

Dreams can be weird
Dreams can be scary
But my dream goes like this.
Animals covering all of the streets
Trying to get rockets to go up to the planets, that reeks
They made a rocket and accomplished their dreams
But going up and up until *bang!* Into the moon
Now they come crashing down.
Argh! They land flat-down on a football pitch
Everyone screamed all confused
Stop the game, stop the match
And all the animals ran around
And found the moon that had come crashing down.

Lucas Wilby (10)
Wath C Of E Primary School, Rotherham

The Shooting Star!

It starts when three friends go to bed
All of a sudden they fall asleep
And they fly up to space
Then in the galaxy they see a shooting star
Flying around and around, stars making a ring like Saturn
A comet crashes right into the shooting star and they collide and a black hole starts
Then they wake up in bed in a fright
In the middle of the night
Trying to sleep tight
But it was not like a treat
They had to retreat
It was not a real delight to me.

Harley May-Straw (10)
Wath C Of E Primary School, Rotherham

Catworld

Every night, deep in my mind,
A world pops into my head.
Someplace that makes me feel scared
A place where I feel dared.
Now I wonder,
In my ponder
How did I get here?
Then I see an army rise,
From all different sides.
I decide to pause
As I feel claws
On the end of paws.
I start running for my life
Being chased by a knife.
My mind bounces up and down
My eyes swirl around
I'm home, free and ready for the day.

Leo Rook (10)
Wath C Of E Primary School, Rotherham

Once Upon A Dream

I wake in my book-bed
Something lifts my head
I look out my book-house
I see a book-machine
I'm very keen to see what it means
I walk as I talk to myself
I pause as I feel my feet turn into paws
I was a dog not in my dream
I saw a cat jump over a log
I let out a furious growl
It let out a horrified yowl
It vanished so did I
I came with a boom
I'm a spoon
I awake in my bed
It was all a dream.

Lily Tyler (9)
Wath C Of E Primary School, Rotherham

Spoon And Me

I see a starry night,
With the hills so bright,
With nobody in sight.
I see the glistening moon,
And I listen to its tune.
I grab my hat,
And set off with my cat.
On the way,
I see cats sway,
Like hay,
And scream, "Yay!"
I get to the moon,
And hear a *boom*,
Soon I see a spoon,
It looms over me.
Who says it is a she,
We become friends,
Spoon and me.

Harry Thompson (9)
Wath C Of E Primary School, Rotherham

The Dragon Realm

I wake up, about to say hi,
But then I see dragons in the sky.
I now know I'm not in my room,
All I know is I'm not in doom.
I'm in a mystic land,
There are dragons, it is grand.
I ride my pet dragon at the speed of light,
He can beat a bad dragon in a fight.
My pet dragon is supersized,
Watch him fly across the skies.
I wish I could always stay,
But I have to start my day.

Luke Coxon (9)
Wath C Of E Primary School, Rotherham

Aliens Take Over

In my dreams late at night,
I see something through the light, *bang!*
I land on a planet called Kepler-22B,
I look all around me and I see little aliens,
I also see they are turquoise and they have one eye,
I also see they had some pie,
Then I was grabbed by the aliens,
I was put in an ice cream cone,
I was put in a dome of a castle,
And I saw a sign that said *Death Zone.*

Sebastian Platts (10)
Wath C Of E Primary School, Rotherham

Once Upon A Dream Of Sheffield United

What a good day,
I'm breath-taken and I have no words to say,
I'm at Bramwell Lane,
And I'm so happy it's like I'm seeing Harry Kane.
What a wonderful joyful sound so clappy,
As the fans are all reluctant to go home,
We are ready to lift the Premier League Cup,
As Chris Wilder (the manager) is ready for his close-up,
I just want to say,
Hip hip hooray!

Louis Edwards (9)
Wath C Of E Primary School, Rotherham

Gameshow

G aming in the moonlit night,
A re you gonna be the one to take on the fight?
M agnificent levels you must pass,
E volving sky high,
S haring your skills to the class,
H ow will you do it because I can't deny, to say you competed with ease sounds like a lie,
O h wow, this is hard,
W ait until we get through Asgard.

Isobel Phillips (10)
Wath C Of E Primary School, Rotherham

The Moon

In the night,
The moon lit bright,
I listen to the tune of the moon.
It sings a short, slow song,
And the birds sing along,
With a boom I zoom to the moon.
I see stars flashing and dashing,
A massive castle walks about.
I feel a lizard crawl on my foot.
Suddenly I pounce up,
I walk to school and see the lizard and nearly scream.

Blake Stone (10)
Wath C Of E Primary School, Rotherham

Alien Friends

I see aliens getting out of their ship
Ready to make friends with me.
The aliens and my family have a picnic
In a big field of flowers,
I am happy and cheerful
As I play with the aliens.
When sunset came,
They said goodbye,
Got on their spaceship,
And drifted away.
They said they'll come back
Again; next year.

Alicia Henderson (9)
Wath C Of E Primary School, Rotherham

In The Sewers

In the sewers below your feet
There is someone for you to meet
Creeping quietly down below
There is a secret you don't know
Sad, cold, full of despair
Which you cannot bear
Even if he tried to get out
There's always a doubt
Seeing feet all up there
Getting angry every day
You wake up and see you're there.

Jacob Smith (9)
Wath C Of E Primary School, Rotherham

If A Cloud Is Strong

It was an afternoon
I just got ready down on the ground
And then got into an aeroplane
To get to a cloud to play football
The only people that could come
Were your family and the fans
And they all feel happy and playful
And everyone likes you
And you become popular
And the clouds are made out of cotton candy.

Finley Cole (9)
Wath C Of E Primary School, Rotherham

Monsters

Can you imagine monsters taking over the blue cheese world,
Can you imagine red pants that'll make you fly in the cheesy sky,
Can you imagine in the night, fighting for your life,
Or ducking your head under your bed?
If you don't, you may get a fright,
And that'll be a horrible sight.

Sonny Blood (9)
Wath C Of E Primary School, Rotherham

Once Upon A Dream

There was a girl in her bed
To lay down her sweet head
Her teddy, Cinnamon Roll
He's not like coal
Flying up high
Right into the sky
With a wish and a whoosh
It makes a sploosh
With a throw of a penny Cinnamon Roll makes a wish
With a glance, she sees a fish.

Maddie Boothroyd (9)
Wath C Of E Primary School, Rotherham

Koala's Stealing The Moon

In my dreams every night,
Koalas steal the moon,
Koalas are just animals, right?
But every night the koalas take flight,
To the moon, they go.
The koalas make a fight,
The moon fights back,
Who will win?
Finally, the koalas win,
They take the moon back to Earth.

Seb Dunn (10)
Wath C Of E Primary School, Rotherham

Pokémon Land

Once upon a time
I was in a Pokémon Land
Everywhere I look around
It's full of Pokémon
Ash, the trainer, is there too
But my favourite is Pikachu
I was amazed and happy
When the Pokémon evolved
My dreams come true in Pokémon Land.

Freddie Bell (10)
Wath C Of E Primary School, Rotherham

In The North Pole

In the North Pole, the cool, thin ice is colder than the sun, which is pleasant.
My cold toes are like snow.
Santa is the best at giving presents.
We leave cookies and milk for Santa on Christmas night as a way to express gratitude for the gifts that Santa brings.

Keelan Nkomo (9)
Wath C Of E Primary School, Rotherham

Motorbike Land

Motorbikes zoom with a vroom
As Harry Potter puts one on his broom.
They won't go out without a boom
As the riders get a bit of doom.
Some of them go into a tomb
As they see dead bodies in a boom
They hear someone singing a tune.

Owen Hanson (9)
Wath C Of E Primary School, Rotherham

In My Dreams

In my dreams, I can see
Buzzy bees with big feet
Monsters eat lobsters
As well as Bobsters
Goblins fly by with no colours
Bright, sparkling horses go by in the night
Dragons roar in the sky
A flying pirate ship whooshes by.

Brody Buck (10)
Wath C Of E Primary School, Rotherham

On Olympus

I go up the elevator so high in the sky
As I get a sudden urge I'm going to die
I look out the window
And see something start to fly
I eventually reach the top
But something goes pop
I see a cook roasting a duck.

Thomas Pearson (9)
Wath C Of E Primary School, Rotherham

My Imaginary Friend Who Ran Away

My imaginary friend, Mr Nobody, ran away
Today, I am sad unlike my dad.
He mopped, chopped, clopped all day long.
Mr Nobody ran away yesterday
And now works at the dock and mops, shops
But I can still hear the clop.

Alexander Brough (9)
Wath C Of E Primary School, Rotherham

A Little Itch

A girl wakes up with a little itch,
Tickling her face,
Her best friend, Stitch,
Is playing some music on his violin,
As I run to school
With Stitch, I start getting an itch.

Jorgie Auckland (9)
Wath C Of E Primary School, Rotherham

A Dream About Hogwarts!

A fun sleepover at my house,
Everything's quiet as a mouse.
When suddenly at my door,
A letter is placed upon the floor.
"A snowy owl!" I squealed with glee,
"A snowy owl, don't make it flee!"
When said the letter, "Follow me."
A howler, it must be!
Later that day,
I yelled, "Hooray!"
For we were at Hogwarts
A misty school
Where a three-headed dog called Fluffy
Was really rather cool.
We swam across the cold, black lake
But that had been a grave mistake.
For when I woke up,
My heart was beating,
And 'twas my PJs I was eating!

It's just a stupid dream, I thought.
I was wrong. Dreams rule!

Rosie Ibbo (9)
West End Primary And Nursery School, Horsforth

Dreams Are In Your Mind For Life

D oing things for family
R eally makes you happy.
E verywhere you
A re because things
M ake you
S mile when you're on tiles.

A ll my dreams are clean when they
R oam my mind
E very time.

I love hugs in the
N ice world.

Y ou all spend the end
O n our Earth.
U p is where I went
R eally it is true.

M y dream is not done
I went to the sun and saw a
N ew world.
D oing their work.

F airy, I was one too.
O utstanding things
R eally, it is true.

L iked every bit
I t was amazing I was a
F airy of everything I had a year here.
E nd when I send a letter.

Lia Brewitt (9)
West End Primary And Nursery School, Horsforth

Going To Space

G od, there are so many weird planets, let's explore.
O h no, where should I go first?
I know, why don't I go to the nonsense planets?
N onsense Planet, why is that a thing? Be, bo, ba, bo, okay, bye
G arden Planet! I should have brought my trowel, this can't get any worse!

T oo bad! Yes, it can!
O h, this one is boring!

S pace, what else will go wrong?
P izza! Yum, is there a dessert?
A nd there is!
C andyland! There are candy cane houses and iced sugar for food!
E verything is now over?

Emily Berry (9)
West End Primary And Nursery School, Horsforth

Transforming Storm

Once there was a witch who had a horrible itch.
She went upon her way, scratching all day.
Once there were two girls, who were full of whirls.
They met on a bridge and then had drinks from a fridge.
Next, they went to their hut, which inside had some nuts.
They made a band, which grew to be grand.
When they made their magic, something always went tragic.
The girls, who were full of whirls.
Changed and transformed when they were bored.
The witch cackled loudly, "Fooled you all!"
Then went to brawl, "I fooled you all!"

Pia Terry (9)
West End Primary And Nursery School, Horsforth

A Premier League Football Player

M an of the Match
A nd never misses a shot on goal!
N ational team will win!
C ross the ball in for a player to score...
H eader the ball into the net.
E nd of the half...
S uper-loud fans
T oday, we will win the treble!
E nd of the season,
R ed, red, red!

U nited we stand,
N ow go you Reds...
I love you, Man U!
T rue to my Reds.
E nd of the Champions League,
D on't let the cross in - and we score!

Seth Morton (9)
West End Primary And Nursery School, Horsforth

Mini Hot Dog Wars

M otorway wars are usual
I ntelligent little hot dogs aren't usual
N ever say they're not cute
I sobel trying to stop it from raging on.

H osepipe disaster went on
O n the road, it is happening,
T oads invaded.

D ogs are good to stop it
O dd one mustard.
G one bonkers!

W ars are bad!
A rmy lost
R oller coaster war!
S and away!

Freya Gawthorpe (9)
West End Primary And Nursery School, Horsforth

Roller Coasters

R ide them
O ver the trees.
L eave the station and
L et yourself be lifted up.
E verlasting memories.
R olling smoothly over

C rowds of people looking
O n with
A we. And you are
S peeding past them.
T he cart is whizzing around all the way
E ven on the loops
R oller coasters, the ultimate experience for you.

Polly Munson (8)
West End Primary And Nursery School, Horsforth

Robot Flying Fire Dragon

It's a robot's fight,
It growls with a fright,
It's like a tank that blasts at enemies,
It's from a different realm far away from home,
It has a lasergun sword like a diamond shield on its back that grows day by day.
It flies and breathes fire everywhere it goes.
What is it?

Answer: A robot dragon that flies and breathes fire out of its cannon, mouth and lasergun sword.

Ryder Kwok (9)
West End Primary And Nursery School, Horsforth

Star Fishing

Get a ladder to the clouds,
Climb and climb all the way up,
Filled with stars, you see a cup,
Get a rod and lower it down.
After a while, you'll claim the stars around,
Fish and fish till you claim a star,
Then you know home isn't far.
The cloud feels like a fluffy delight,
What a simply splendid night.
Catch a ride from the rocky moon,
The next thing you know you'll be home soon.

Isobel Barnes (8)
West End Primary And Nursery School, Horsforth

The Fame Of A Great Dane

Once upon a dream,
My dog was a tween.
Don't worry, she's not mean,
But she is never clean.
Her name is Disco; she always barks,
No! Although she sings solo.
She dances with Taylor Swift
While she does a drift!
Go, Disco! Go!
But mind Madonna's big toe!
Now, put on that pink bow!
Get on a spray tan,
And go on stage with a bang!

Sienna Christou (8)
West End Primary And Nursery School, Horsforth

The Nightmare

I woke up to the warm, summer morning,
Climbed out of bed,
Looked out the window
And to my horror, I saw a
Strange man knocking on my door.
The man stuck a tube-like shape out of his mouth.
He devoured the soul
And the body sunk south.
He looked at me with hunger in his eyes
So I ran down the stairs to see my mum making pies.

Polly Bagnall (9)
West End Primary And Nursery School, Horsforth

The Key To Getting Black Dragon Back

Oh dragon black,
I wish I hadn't thrown you away.
I think you will be in the big black sack.
I feel very black.
I think you will be in a landfill full of black sacks.
I wish you were on my windowsill, but you're in a landfill.
I wish you were never in a landfill.
But you are.
I am feeling upset, sad and angry.

Ethan Taylor (9)
West End Primary And Nursery School, Horsforth

Blackburn

B lackburn Rovers,
L oud chanting fans.
A lways my team,
C orners are the dream!
K icking winners,
B all in the net,
U nbelievable team!
R overs are great; nothing to beat.
N ever think it's over; we always win...

Because we are Blackburn Rovers.

Harry Pearson (9)
West End Primary And Nursery School, Horsforth

Dream, The XC Horse

My lovely little Dream
Who is never, ever mean,
Who also loves Mr Bean
And she's never quite clean.
She loves to set the scene
And makes the crowd beam.
Now this little Dream is very special
And she will never settle.
At the XC course where she eats Hesal
As she jumps the petal.

Holly Adams (9)
West End Primary And Nursery School, Horsforth

Panda

I once saw a panda as fluffy as could be,
It had black and white fur that glistened with glee.
My mum was there with blondish hair
And mumbled, "What's this mess?"
I got up from my big, green seat
And listened to where it sleeps.
"It claimed it sleeps in a big green bean!"

Ayda Solhan (9)
West End Primary And Nursery School, Horsforth

The Footballer

M an of the Match every week,
A nd scores every time,
N ever missing a free kick.

C arrying the team in the Champions League
I can win the Ballon d'Or.
T hey call him the best footballer in the world.
Y ou can win the treble with your team.

Josh Wheat (9)
West End Primary And Nursery School, Horsforth

Man United

M an of the Match
A nd never gets a red card
N ever going home feeling sad

U nited unite people
N ationals
I t gives you the feeling of a man
T orture in every game
E lated at Old Trafford
D elivering the goals.

Dylan Thorpe (8)
West End Primary And Nursery School, Horsforth

Robodog

My dream is quite mean,
He is quite clean and also likes Mr Bean.
He is Robodog, I usually give him a log
To happily chew on.
He likes watching ping-pong.
He likes it when the door goes ding-dong.
I found him in a hidden chest
And he surely looks the best.

Charlie Buckle (8)
West End Primary And Nursery School, Horsforth

Becoming A Lego Designer

I want to be a Lego designer,
My dream couldn't be finer.

I want to make the fans happy,
I want to make them yappy.

We have to work as a team,
We can't be mean.

And one day, my dream could come true,
Yes, it may!

Jacob Barker (8)
West End Primary And Nursery School, Horsforth

Man United

M an of the Match
A nd scores lots of goals.
N ew players.

U nited
N ever misses a goal.
I 'm a red.
T akes chances.
E very game I get better.
D eafening crowd.

Jack Hollowood (9)
West End Primary And Nursery School, Horsforth

Robucks

Right now, Roblox is my favourite game,
Everyone can play super fun games - there are lots!
Today, my happy daddy allowed me to get £50 of Robucks and that is lots!
I spent it on lots of specific, random stuff on my favourite game of all.

Elliot Johnson (9)
West End Primary And Nursery School, Horsforth

Candyland

One night I drifted off to sleep
I woke up in my dream,
And saw a doughnut queen.
She was dressed from head to toe in dripping chocolate drizzles.
Her shoes were made of strawberry laces,
But they did not look very stable.

Charlotte Wood (9)
West End Primary And Nursery School, Horsforth

Rabbit Hole

Once upon a time,
I fell down a rabbit hole
And into a pole,
But landed in Candyland,
And there was a band.
There was a lady,
Singing about a jelly baby.
There was a guitar,
That was a star.

Liv Gallagher (8)
West End Primary And Nursery School, Horsforth

Dreamy Read

Once upon a dreamy read
There was a boy
He whispered a riddle.
"What's bigger when you subtract from it,
And what gets smaller when you add to it?"

Answer: A hole!

Toby Bagnall (9)
West End Primary And Nursery School, Horsforth

Man U

M anchester always win their matches
A aron Wan-Bissaka carries the team.
N ever lose a match,

U nited love to win in their red kit.

Charlie Banks (8)
West End Primary And Nursery School, Horsforth

Piggy Pet

P recious little piggy
I ntelligent and kind
G raceful but greedy
G ertrude eats all the time
Y um, yum, in my tum, Mum!

Ellen Procter (9)
West End Primary And Nursery School, Horsforth

I Have A Pet Tiger

T rembling but cool,
I ntelligent, clean.
G iant and kind,
E ncouraging and funny.
R avishing and also shines. Stripy!

Florence Hoult (8)
West End Primary And Nursery School, Horsforth

My Dream Dog

Dogs
Brown, orange
Labrador called Poppy.
Barking in every direction.
Panting.

Reuben Barker (8)
West End Primary And Nursery School, Horsforth

The Football Soldier

Jake
Army soldier
Plays football, Leeds
His aim is good
Jake.

Jake Petty (9)
West End Primary And Nursery School, Horsforth

YOUNG WRITERS INFORMATION

We hope you have enjoyed reading this book – and that you will continue to in the coming years.

If you're a young writer who enjoys reading and creative writing, or the parent of an enthusiastic poet or story writer, do visit our website **www.youngwriters.co.uk**. Here you will find free competitions, workshops and games, as well as recommended reads, a poetry glossary and our blog.

If you would like to order further copies of this book, or any of our other titles, then please give us a call or visit **www.youngwriters.co.uk**.

Young Writers
Remus House
Coltsfoot Drive
Peterborough
PE2 9BF
(01733) 890066
info@youngwriters.co.uk

YoungWritersUK YoungWritersCW
youngwriterscw youngwriterscw